LIBBY MCKECHNIE

 FriesenPress

One Printers Way
Altona, MB R0G 0B0
Canada

www.friesenpress.com

Copyright © 2024 by Libby McKechnie
First Edition — 2024

All rights reserved.

No part of this publication may be reproduced in any form, or by any means, electronic or mechanical, including photocopying, recording, or any information browsing, storage, or retrieval system, without permission in writing from FriesenPress.

ISBN
978-1-03-832074-2 (Hardcover)
978-1-03-832073-5 (Paperback)
978-1-03-832075-9 (eBook)

1. POETRY, CANADIAN

Distributed to the trade by The Ingram Book Company

For my parents, George and Clare, and my sister, Jody
I hold so much of you in my heart.

Contents

Great Blue Heron	4
Monet's Giverny	6
The Island	8
Snapshots of Santa Fe	10
A Toast to Marc Chagall	12
Snow, Rain, Puddles, and Mist	14
Life Lessons	16
Hands	18
Harbingers	20
Aren't They Beautiful	22
Starlight	24
Too Many Dishes of Fish	26
No Words Needed	28
Poppy	30
Calm Waters	32
Rain	34
The Ents	36
Frigid Beauty	38
Open Window	40
Cloud Mirror	42
Interconnected	44
Petra	46
Meditation	48
Hearts	50
Acknowledgements	52
About the Author	53

Great Blue Heron

He lands in front of me
gently touching down
in the long grasses
along the shoreline
he doesn't seem to mind
my sitting close by
or my admiration
for his regal beauty
and sudden
commanding presence
with his tremendous
fanned out wings
and long, sword-like beak
as he wades into
the small marsh
and just as quickly
disappears

Monet's Giverny

I walked to the Musée de l'Orangerie
in Paris to see Monet's waterlilies

after sitting for some time
with these beautiful paintings

I knew I must visit Giverny
Monet's home and flower gardens

standing on his Japanese bridge
overlooking his water lily pond

walking through many flower gardens
I finally understood

Monet saw all this vibrant colour
in his gardens, water, and sky

he was able to capture how colour
changes with the light

in both his landscapes and waterlily paintings
something magical and soul expanding happens

when you have the time to sit and really see

The Island

At Ballynahinch castle in Connemara
I walked across a bridge to a small island
where a few palm trees and other
large tropical plants created a lush
private oasis. A worn wooden bench
faced the river, a hidden place to sit
and breathe in all this beauty.
Later, as I walked the path along
the river's edge I saw many small
bright pink, purple, and white flowers
growing among leafy ferns.
I could smell the dampness of fallen leaves
a faint spicy fragrance from the surrounding woods.
The old tree trunks had thick carpets
of kelly-green moss cascading down the sides.
I suddenly had a strong intuition
that a tiny woodland elf
or a flower fairy might be watching me.
In this very old magical place
I knew I was not alone.

Snapshots of Santa Fe

Wandering travellers look for inspiration
hope to discover beauty
in and out of art galleries boasting
sculpture in glass and bronze
and colourful, contemporary paintings
unique silver jewelry displayed
in the central market square
ranch houses along each street
low stone walls surrounding them
open courtyards with patterned, wrought-iron gates
huge pots of red-and-pink geraniums placed
by benches or chairs painted blue or green
every day the sky is a beautiful turquoise
the sun always shining
the Sangre de Cristo Mountains
silhouetted in the distance
this desert town has beauty to spare

A Toast to Marc Chagall

You moved to Paris as a young man.
Sometimes your paintings were like a dream
your bride and you, floating
on air along with the Eiffel tower.
Dreams do happen in Paris, a magical,
inspiring city where painters come
to experiment with new ideas. Who but you
could paint a cow, a chicken, and a violinist
playing on a rooftop. You designed stained-glass
windows, costumes for the ballet, murals for the opera.
I raise my glass of Sauvignon Blanc to toast you.
To Paris. I always long to return.

Snow, Rain, Puddles, and Mist

Umbrella in hand
I walk on snow-cleared roads
rain falling and splashing
melting winter ice
dark tree branches
reflect in the puddles
winter beauty, white snow
fog and mist hovering among the trees
it's like walking on the moors in *Jane Eyre*
I wait for an apparition of some kind
then rein in my imagination
and continue on my way
wondering if we can become more
like trees that flourish in all kinds
of weather and changes
to their surroundings

Life Lessons

I remember when I was nine
driving home with you from Holmes school.
You suddenly turned the car around
while telling me the class pet
was still sitting in the doll highchair.
We needed to return to your kindergarten
classroom to put it in its cage.
You didn't sound upset
simply explained the situation.

Another time I watched you on stage
at a school assembly
speaking clearly and calmly
into a microphone.
You were addressing everyone
in the entire school.
I felt so proud that you were my mom.

Sometimes we'd go shopping together
on Saturday.
You told me to choose clothes
that I liked so I would enjoy wearing them.
We'd have lunch at Henrici's
and strawberry cheesecake
which was so delicious.
You never made me feel like
I disappointed you, just let me be
myself and that was enough.

I thought of you
on New Year's eve
I ordered cheesecake with berries
so delicious.

Hands

Gentle hands smoothing my special silk pyjamas.

Strong hands lifting me up to the drawer
to smell her gift soaps and choose one for my bath.

Creative hands gently bouncing my mattress
to help me fall asleep.

Practical hands brushing her hair and rolling it up
around an elastic band to keep it off her neck.

Calloused hands putting on white gloves
carefully rolling up her nylon stockings.

Busy hands baking delicious large sugar cookies.

Caring hands helping me stir my favourite
raspberry custard on the stove.

Grandma's loving hands always holding me tight
at every single coming and going.

Harbingers

On March break I left winter white
to be thrust into North Carolina's
early green, its soft floral fragrances.
Pink crab apple trees growing all along
the parkway, moving up and over
the mountainside.
Purple crocuses popping up around
forsythia bushes' bright yellow.
It's hard not to feel cheerful.
Spring always surprises me,
the way it welcomes me home.

Aren't They Beautiful

"Look at all those colours. Aren't they beautiful?"
my dad would say. Two large wire flight cages on wheels
housed his hundred parakeets chattering away.
Our glassed-in back porch had large, sun-filled
windows, a happy place for birdwatching.

All concerns suspended
as we watched the birds preen, flap
their wings in the water dish to cool off,
hang upside down on stick perches.

"Hold out your hand," he said. "Be very gentle."
We stood next to a nest box where
eggs had just hatched. A naked,
pink, tiny bird with its huge eyes still closed
gently placed in my hand.

I looked down in complete wonder
at this amazing, warm, breathing creature.
This was a huge gift for a small girl,
to hold for just a moment
one of his precious baby birds.

Starlight

In my dream
he ran up to me
laughing
a small boy
his eyes sparkling
with the joy of play
back then
I was his North Star
his guiding light
the centre of his universe
he is a man now
with his own concerns
and responsibilities
I will always shine
in his heaven
but now
as one of many
other stars
on the periphery
of his galaxy

Too Many Dishes of Fish

Travelling around Ireland
local fish were on the menu:
hake, halibut, haddock, salmon
sea bass, pollack, pike, and perch
trout, turbot, mussels, and flounder.
One night a small local restaurant
offered a simple pasta dish with chicken
and mushrooms in marinara sauce.
I could have danced on the table
and sung to the chef
with my glass of Pinot Grigio.
The next day I was ready
for even more delicious dishes of fish.

No Words Needed

A small girl and her dog
sit together side by side
looking out at the world
in innocence and wonder
in the stillness of early morning
these two have a special bond
their own unspoken communication
they begin each day as best pals
just waiting for an adventure

Poppy

I always look for you
your dazzling red face
lifted toward the sun
you stand out among all
the other flowers in the garden
on windy days you sway
on your tall stem
like a singer with a microphone
owning the stage and
the entire audience

Calm Waters

a few leaves drift down and float along a stream, soft raindrops create circles on the surface
a deeper pool of water reveals spring-green moss on rocks underneath patches of topaz
yellow and azure blue, a large leaf floats, spins, partially submerges, caught on something
listening to water lazily trickling over rocks I suddenly take in a deep breath and realize
how very peaceful I feel

Rain

Torrents streaming down roof gutters
Pattering on porch roof
Drops pinging off my umbrella
Silver needles dancing on asphalt
Rivulets running along curbs
Puddles soaking my running shoes
Splashes quickly filling a birdbath
Spherical drops balancing on leaf edges
My five-year-old self reminds me
Why I love rain
I happily splash my way home

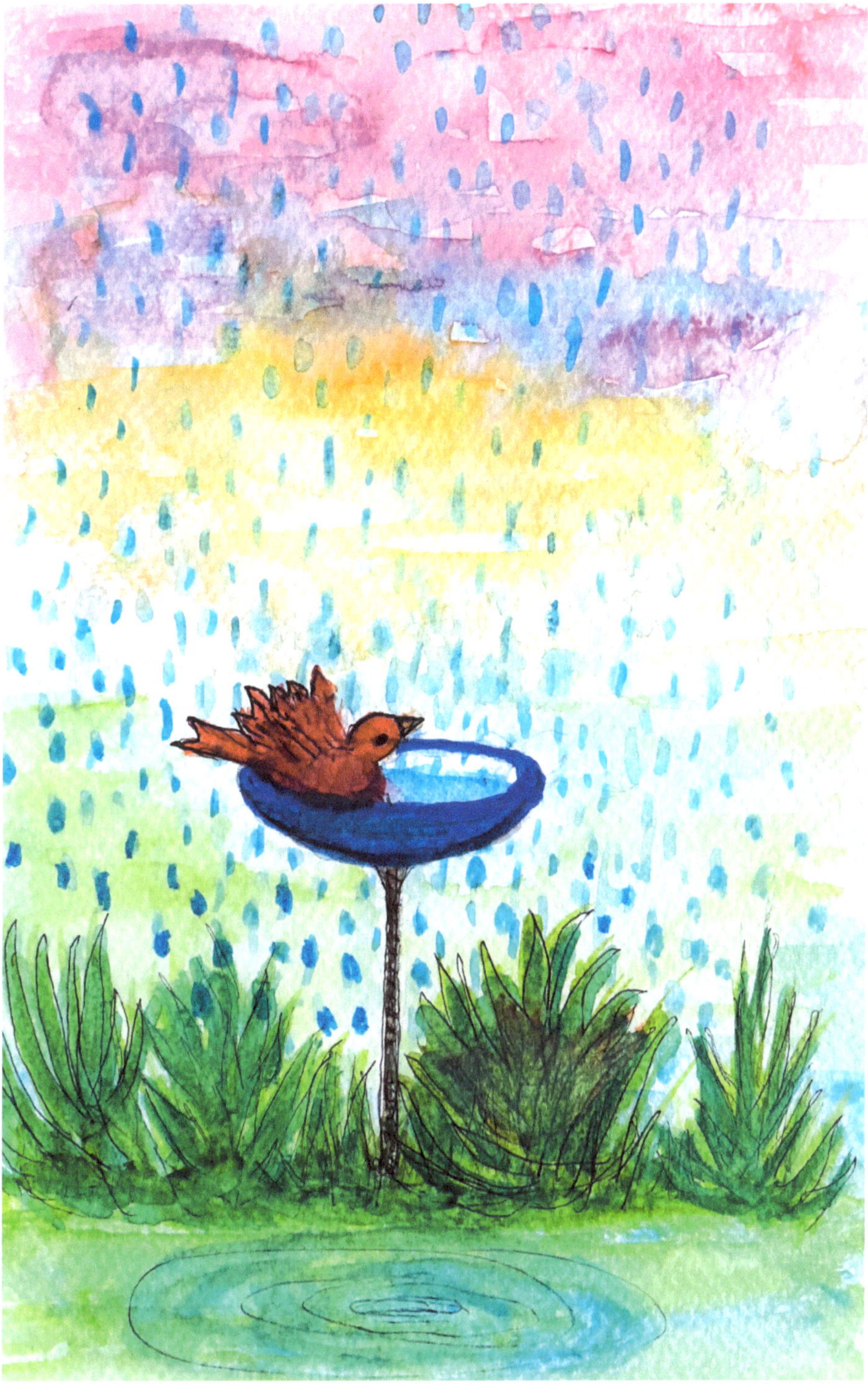

The Ents

High up in the branches of one of these huge old trees
I experience power and quiet authority
with which they inhabit their world, clomping
down the forest hillside in loping strides.
I hold on tighter, listening through the rustling leaves
to the ancient language the trees speak to each other,
their low, calm voices. The creaking and groaning
of swaying branches alerts me to the fact that I am
only a visitor to their ancient world. They have existed
for centuries. They will continue to grow
and change. Looking up through sun-filtering branches
I feel grateful. These living entities that model
adaptation so well. Though over time they become ancient
still remain wise.

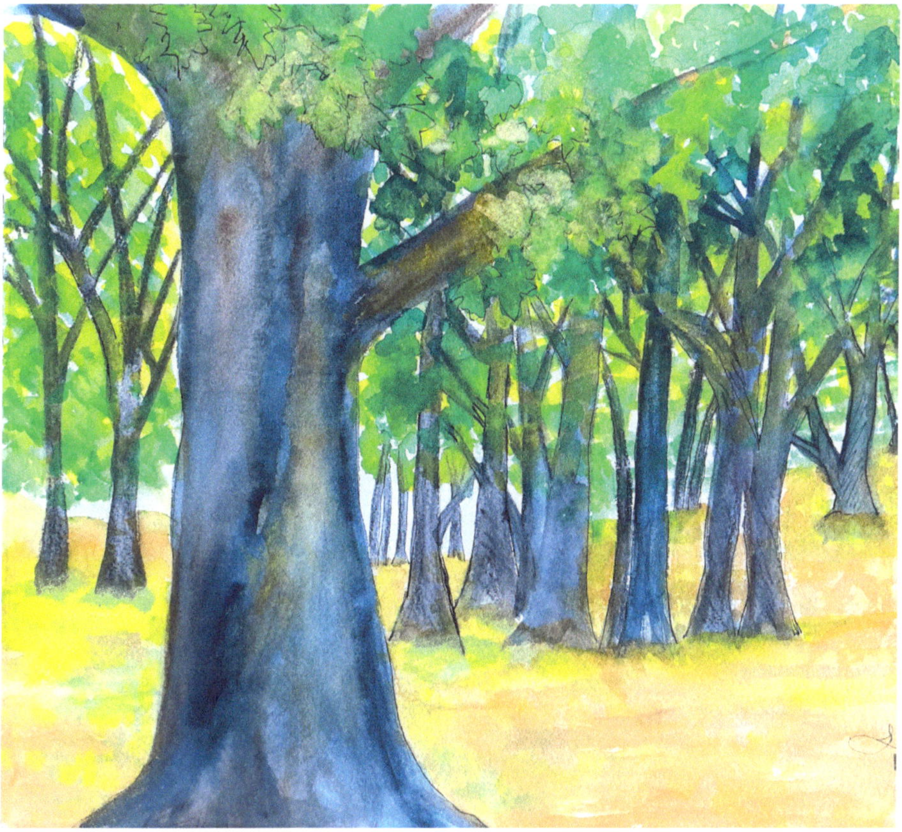

Frigid Beauty

Cold air wakes up my brain
I alternate hands in my coat pockets

Snow crunching underfoot
a blue jay's call, distinct and shrill

Dark green cedar hedges upholstered
in textured white

Bare branches reach skyward in praise
tall pines, branches heavy with soft mounds

A crow cawing loudly from the tip-top
sunshine and shadow chasing each other

From tree to tree and across fields of white
tiny trees glittering in frost on my garage window

I find the shape of myself in the hard beauty
of a winter morning

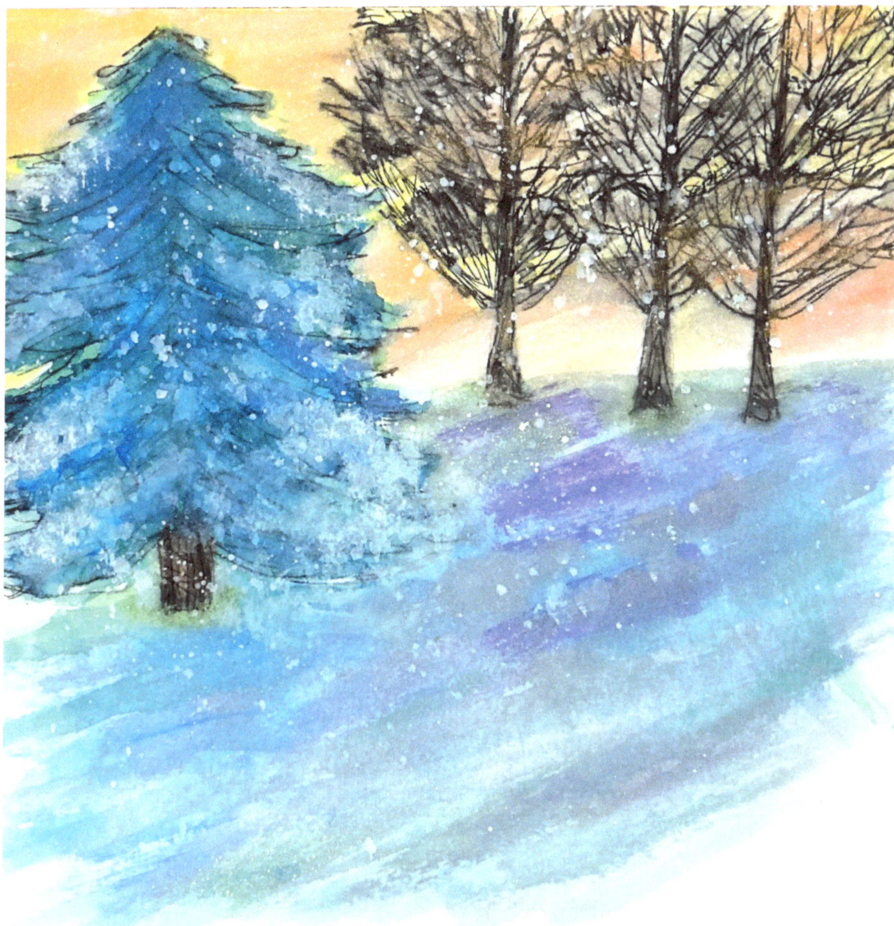

Open Window

When the night air softly
enters my open window
it brings dreams

of great grey owls
coasting through the trees
on powerful wings, softly feathered

and noiseless. Small animals
are tucked tight inside logs
or ground nests, cuddled together

sheltered and warm.
Songbirds keep hidden in high nests
with fluffed-out downy feathers.

In my dream, I too glide
on feathered wings
looking down over trees

undulating hills and rivers
awakened by moonlight,
feeling this cool night air

surrounding me
lifting me, holding me up.
I ride the wings of darkness

until the sun begins its climb.

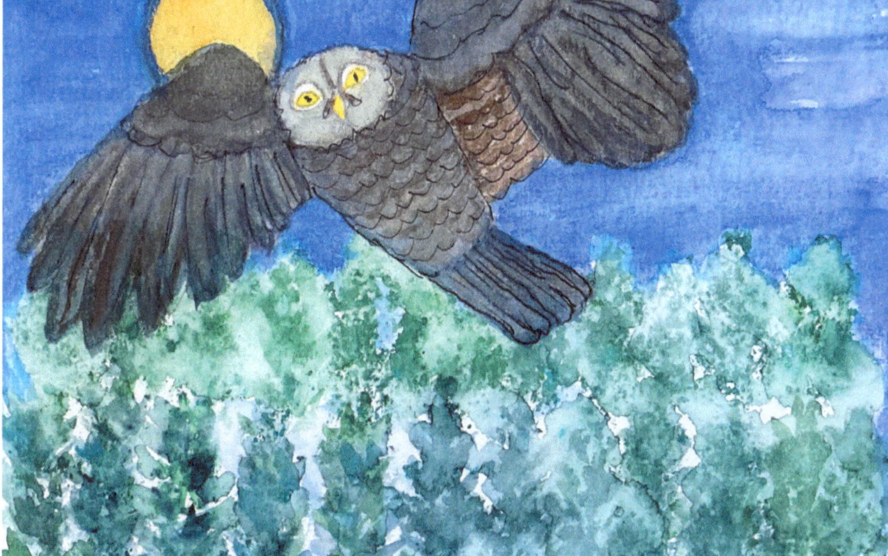

Cloud Mirror

Light and dark clouds
sometimes appear together
on the surface of the water

so like us and our emotions
bright with sunlight some days
dark and brooding on others

waves rippling calm exteriors
during high winds
rainstorms dumping on us

we hold on inching forward slowly
when we least expect it
the sun peeks through

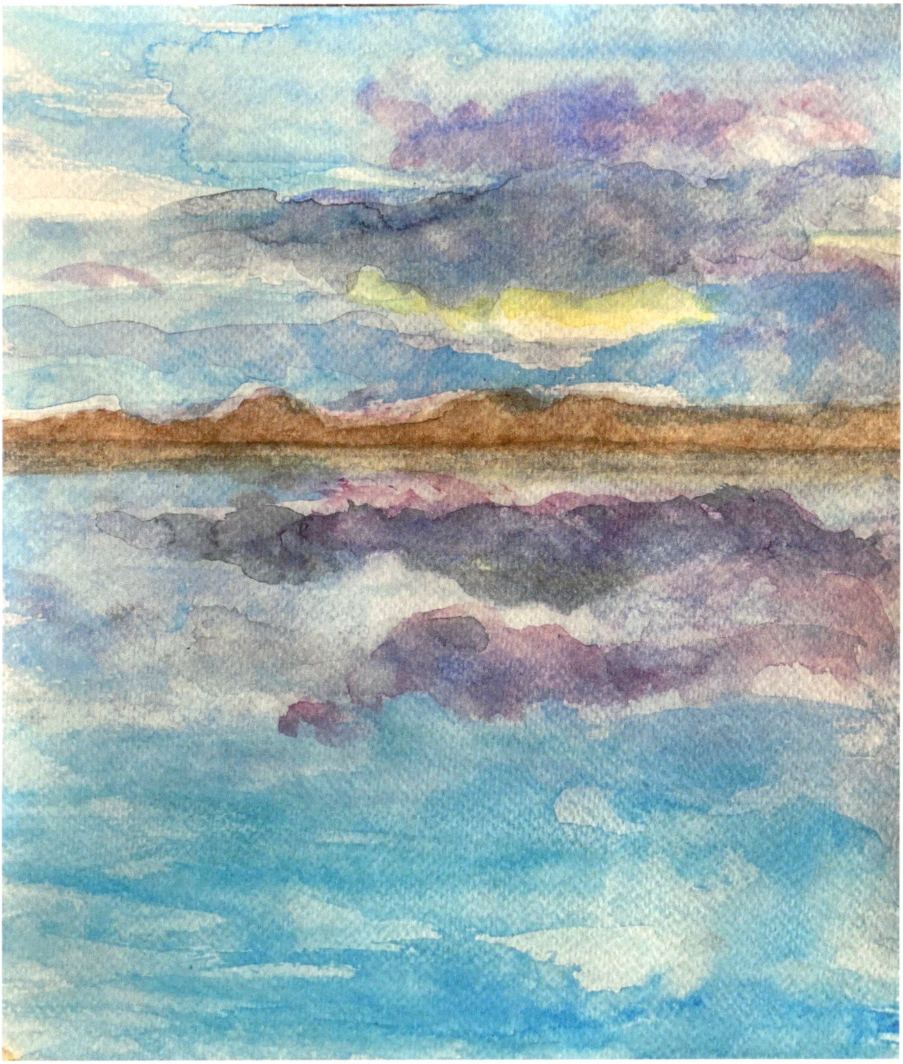

Interconnected

I run my hand along tree branches
touching soft needles of a white pine
breathing in its spicy aroma
sunlight filters through the trees
warming up patches of skin on my face
I walk outside every morning feeling grateful
for the rhythm in my legs
knowing I am connected to the sky
the birds, trees and flowers
I marvel at the colours of cardinal
and bluejay flitting from ground to branch
the song sparrow sings its morning praise
filling me up, starting my day with joy

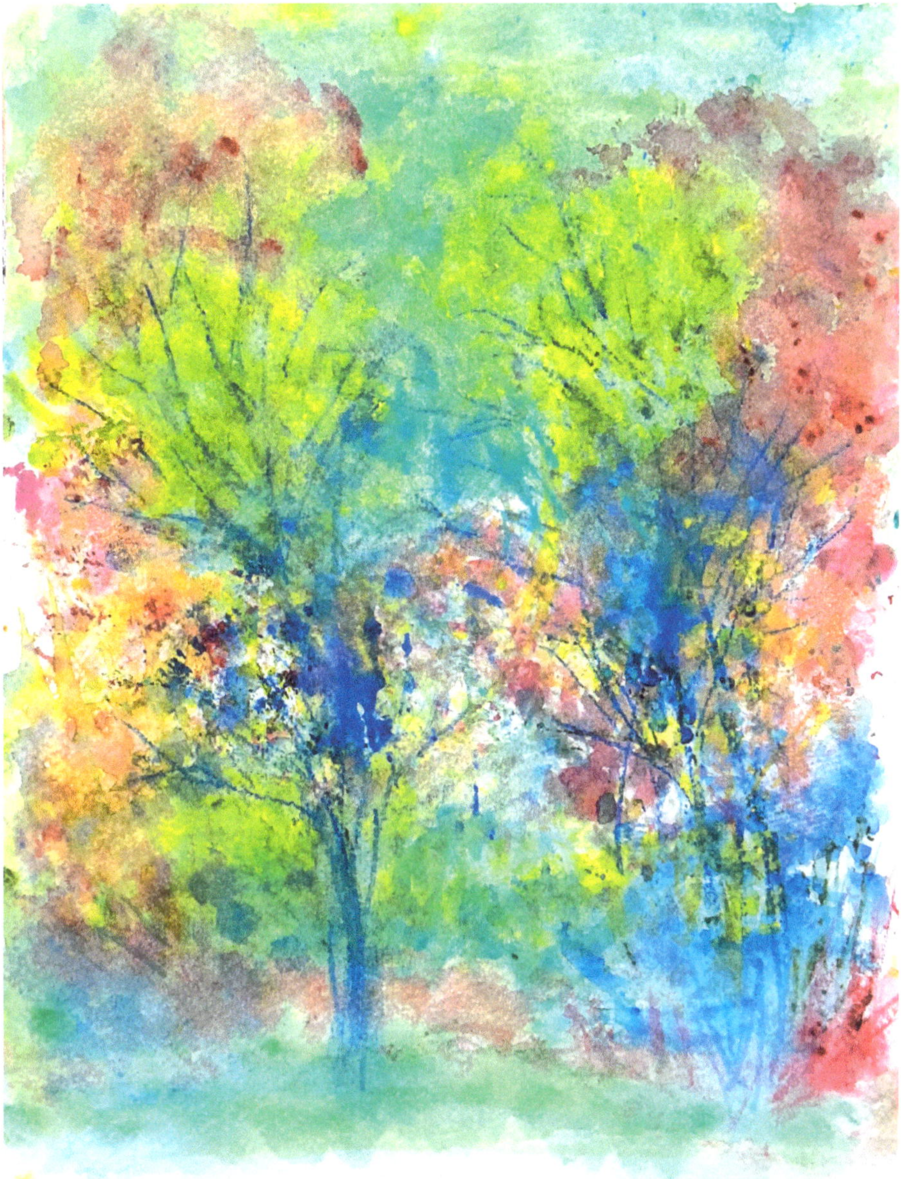

Petra

Once in a lifetime you are lucky to experience
time as it slows down then stands still.
An ancient city in a desert valley in Jordan
can only be entered through a magnificent gorge.
Rose-coloured sandstone twists and turns for almost two miles
until on foot, donkey cart, or camel, you turn the corner
into history. A pristine, white, classical temple
built into the rock wall. Perched up in the clouds
is a monastery with many stairs and levels to climb up
to the entrance. Beautifully carved tombs of past kings
who once reigned here are placed throughout the city.
Once a thriving centre for trade and commerce
this ancient place has been resilient over time. So well preserved.
It is impossible not to be changed by being here
a small part of its history.

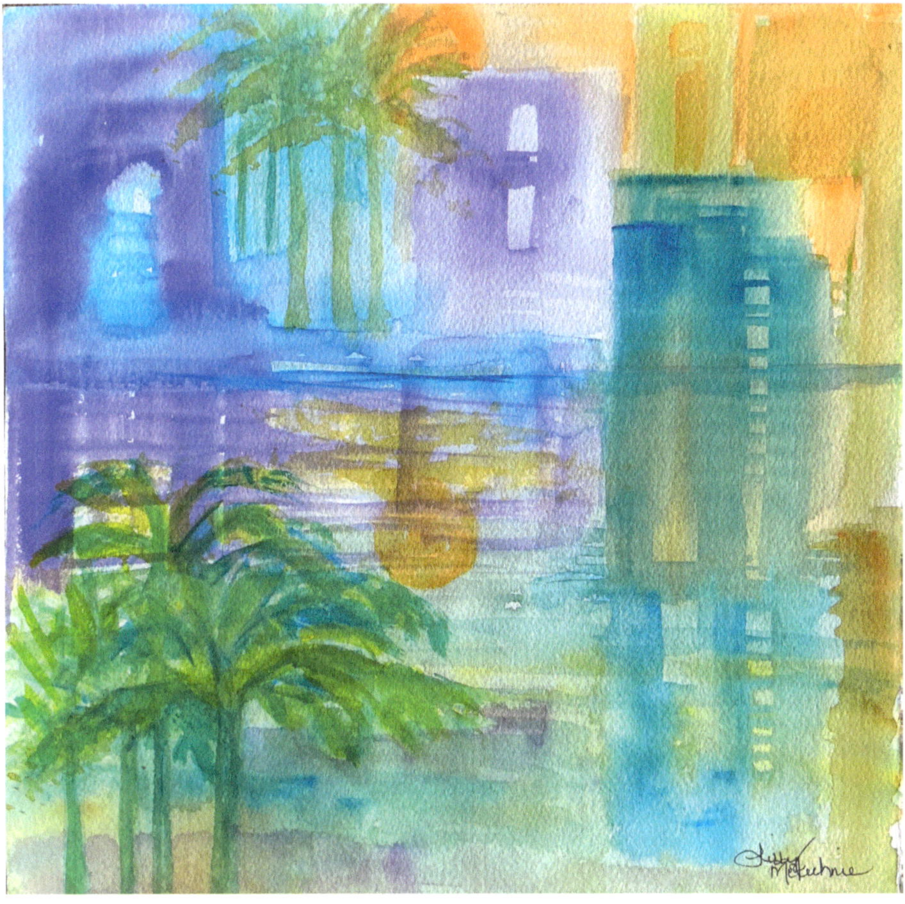

Meditation

Across the river the sky is a kaleidoscope.
Thin purple-and-grey wisps of clouds slowly float
across white, puffy shapes backlit
by yellow sunshine in a blue sky,
layered, like a watercolour painting.
A cabin cruiser drifts lazily along
cutting small ripples in the reflected landscape.
I listen to the soft lapping of water
against the rocks, wind ruffling the leaves above
and all around me like a whisper,
Be still and know that I am God.

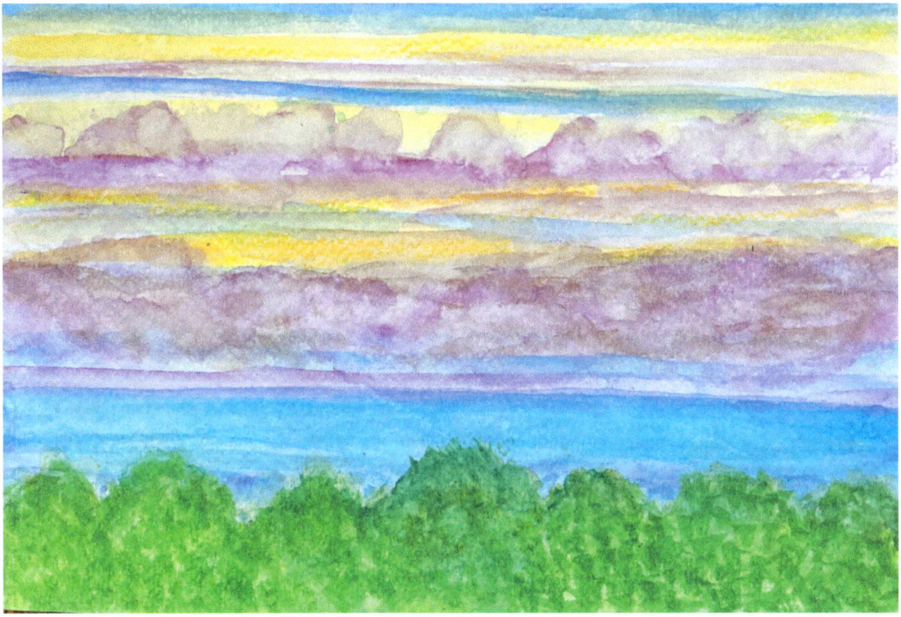

Hearts

From my heart to your heart
from your heart to mine
love is a story
told over time

Life can be fleeting
it can also be long
a purpose and passion
can help us stay strong

Hug those you love
and always be kind
there are so many people
whose lives are not fine

Hearts are so fragile
they can be broken
when hurts and heartaches
remain unspoken

Handle with care
all the hearts that you hold
carefully love them
so they become bold

Our world needs more people
whose hearts can share
love and compassion
and show that they care

From my heart to your heart
from your heart to mine
love is a story
told over time

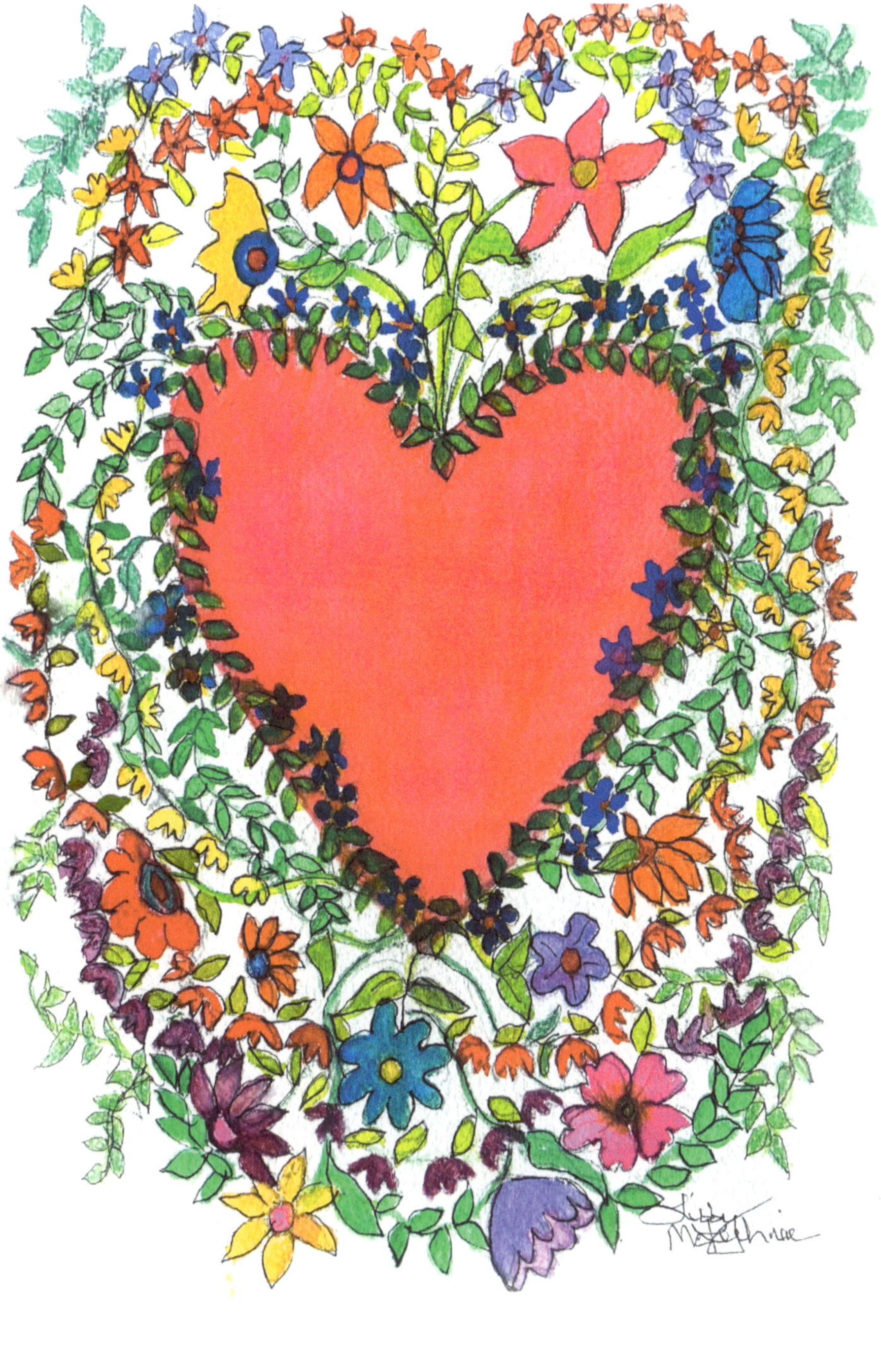

Acknowledgements

I would like to thank my Friesen book editor who encouraged me to rethink and try new ways of seeing and hearing my poetry.

Thank you, Adam, for patiently showing and explaining Microsoft Word so many times.

Thank you, Amy, for being such a gentle, helpful reader when I needed one.

About the Author

Libby McKechnie is a Canadian painter, teacher, and poet. Her debut collection, *Come Away With Me,* was published by FriesenPress in 2021. She has worked as a visual arts teacher in both public and private high schools in Ottawa, Ontario, for more than thirty years, and she also taught in a Montessori school for ten years. A visual artist all her life, poetry came as a form of expression to her later in life, when she began hosting a monthly writing group. For Libby, poetry is the language of the heart, and painting is a visual interpretation of what she sees and feels. She is delighted to be able to share with the world her love of both art and poetry.

Libby lives in Ottawa with her husband. They have two sons and a granddaughter.